Illustrated by
Marisa Vestita

Graphic design
Valentina Giammarinaro

W0010622

WHITE STAR PUBLISHERS

WS White Star Publishers® is a registered trademark
property of White Star s.r.l.

© 2017 White Star s.r.l.
Piazzale Luigi Cadorna, 6
20123 Milan, Italy
www.whitestar.it

Translation: Iceigeo, Milan

ISBN 978-88-544-1121 0
1 2 3 4 5 6   21 20 19 18 17

Printed in Italy by Rotolito Lombarda - Seggiano di Pioltello (MI)

SIZES, MEASUREMENTS AND CONVERSIONS

Women

Shirts

USA	4	6	8	10	12	14
GB	6	8	10	12	14	16
D	32	34	36	38	40	42
F	34	36	38	40	42	44
I	38	40	42	44	46	48

Dresses/Suits

USA	4	6	8	10	12	14
GB	6	8	10	12	14	16
D	32	34	36	38	40	42
F	34	36	38	40	42	44
I	38	40	42	44	46	48

Jeans

USA	4	6	6-8	8-10	10	12
GB	25	27	28	29	30	32
D	25	27	28	29	30	32
F	25	27	28	29	30	32
I	25	27	28	29	30	32

Shoes

USA	6	6½	7½	8½	9	9½
GB	3½	4	5	6	6½	7
D	36	37	38	39	40	41
F	35	36	37	38	39	40
I	36	37	38	39	40	41

Weight
oz = 28.349 g
g = 0.03527 oz
lb = 0.4536 kg
kg = 2.205 lb

Volume
1 (USA) gal = 3.7854 l
0.2642 (USA) gal = 1 l
1 (GB) gal = 4.5460 l
0.2200 (GB) gal = 1 l

Temperature
0 °C = 32 °F

Speed
1 mph = 1.6 km/h

Men

Shirts

USA	14½	15	15½	16	16½	17
GB	14½	15	15½	16	16½	17
D	37	38	39	40	41	42
F	37	38	39	40	41	42
I	37	38	39	40	41	42

Suits/Coats

USA	36	38	40	42	44	46
GB	36	38	40	42	44	46
D	40	42	44	46	48	50
F	42	44	46	48	50	52
I	46	48	50	52	54	56

Jeans

USA	32	33	34	35	36	38
GB	32	33	34	35	36	38
D	32	33	34	35	36	38
F	32	33	34	35	36	38
I	32	33	34	35	36	38

Shoes

USA	8½	9	9½	10	10½	11
GB	8	8½	9	9½	10	10½
D	40	41	42	43	44	45
F	40	41	42	43	44	45
I	40	41	42	43	44	45

Length

1 in = 2.54 cm
0.3937 in = 1 cm
1 SM = 1.6093 km
0.6214 SM = 1 km
1 NM = 1.8519 km
0.5400 NM = 1 km

Area

1 ac = 0.4047 ha
2.471 ac = 1 ha
1 SM² = 2.5900 km²
0.3861 SM² = 1 km²

LANGUAGES AND CURRENCY

Spanish	Argentine peso
English	Australian dollar
German	Euro
French (Walloon), Dutch (Flemish) and German	Euro
Portuguese	Brazilian real
English and French	Canadian dollar
Chinese	Chinese renminbi
Croatian	Croatian kuna
Danish	Danish krone
Finnish and Swedish	Euro
French	Euro
German	Euro
Greek	Euro
Chinese and English	Hong Kong dollar
Hungarian	Hungarian Forint
Hindi and English	Indian rupee
Irish Gaelic and English	Euro
Icelandic	Icelandic króna
Hebrew and Arabic	New shekel
Italian	Euro
Japanese	Japanese yen
Malay	Malaysian ringgit
Spanish	Mexican peso
Dutch and Frisian	Euro
English and Māori	New Zealand dollar
Norwegian	Norwegian krone
Polish	Polish złoty
Portuguese	Euro
Romanian	Romanian leu
Russian	Russian ruble
Slovak	Euro
Slovene, Italian and Hungarian	Euro
English and Afrikaans	South African rand
Korean South	Korean won
Spanish	Euro
Swedish	Swedish krona
German, French, Italian and Romansh	Swiss franc
Turkish	New Turkish lira
English	Pound sterling
English	United States dollar

Argentina	RA	+54	.ar
Australia	AUS	+61	.au
Austria	A	+43	.at
Belgium	B	+32	.be
Brazil	BR	+55	.br
Canada	CDN	+1	.ca
China	CN	+86	.cn
Croatia	HR	+385	.hr
Denmark	DK	+45	.dk
Finland	FIN	+358	.fi
France	F	+33	.fr
Germany	D	+49	.de
Greece	GR	+30	.gr
Hong Kong	HK	+852	.hk
Hungary	H	+36	.hu
India	IND	+91	.in
Ireland	IRL	+353	.ie
Iceland	IS	+354	.is
Israel	IL	+972	.il
Italy	I	+39	.it
Japan	J	+81	.jp
Malaysia	MAL	+60	.my
Mexico	MEX	+52	.mx
Netherlands	NL	+31	.nl
New Zealand	NZ	+64	.nz
Norway	N	+47	.no
Poland	PL	+48	.pl
Portugal	P	+351	.pt
Romania	RO	+40	.ro
Russia	RUS	+7	.ru
Slovakia	SK	+421	.sk
Slovenia	SLO	+386	.si
South Africa	ZA	+27	.za
South Korea	ROK	+82	.kr
Spain	E	+34	.es
Sweden	S	+46	.se
Switzerland	CH	+41	.ch
Turkey	TR	+90	.tr
United Kingdom	GB	+44	.uk
United States of America	USA	+1	.us

TIME ZONES

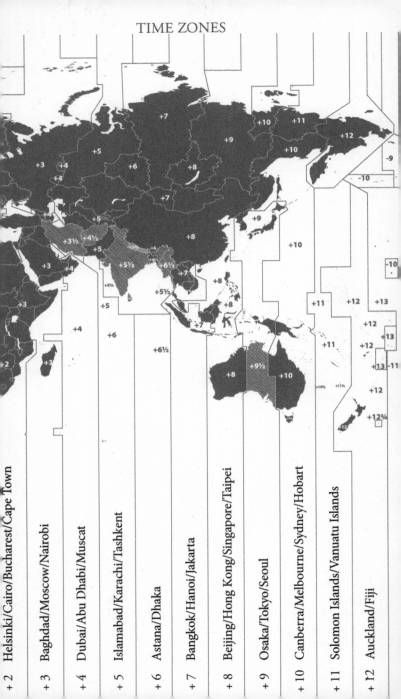

+ 2 Helsinki/Cairo/Bucharest/Cape Town

+ 3 Baghdad/Moscow/Nairobi

+ 4 Dubai/Abu Dhabi/Muscat

+ 5 Islamabad/Karachi/Tashkent

+ 6 Astana/Dhaka

+ 7 Bangkok/Hanoi/Jakarta

+ 8 Beijing/Hong Kong/Singapore/Taipei

+ 9 Osaka/Tokyo/Seoul

+ 10 Canberra/Melbourne/Sydney/Hobart

+ 11 Solomon Islands/Vanuatu Islands

+ 12 Auckland/Fiji

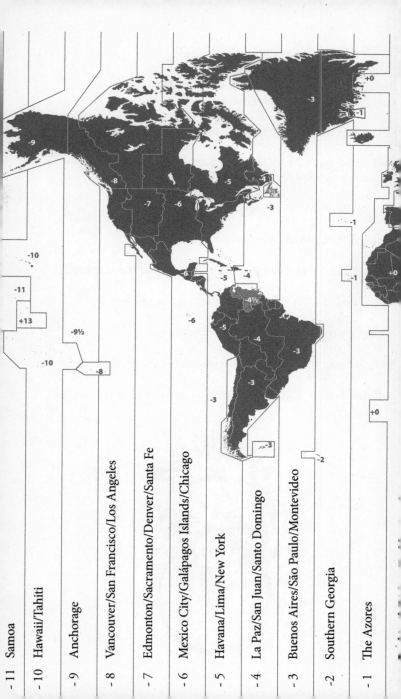

- 11 Samoa

- 10 Hawaii/Tahiti

- 9 Anchorage

- 8 Vancouver/San Francisco/Los Angeles

- 7 Edmonton/Sacramento/Denver/Santa Fe

- 6 Mexico City/Galápagos Islands/Chicago

- 5 Havana/Lima/New York

- 4 La Paz/San Juan/Santo Domingo

- 3 Buenos Aires/São Paulo/Montevideo

- 2 Southern Georgia

- 1 The Azores

Bassani, Giorgio, *1916-2000, Italian writer and poet*

Castellaneta, Carlo, *1930-2013, Italian writer and journalist*

Ceronetti, Guido, *1927-, Italian poet, philosopher, writer and journalist*

Ciampi, Carlo Azeglio, *1920-2016, Italian economist, banker and statesman*

Cordero di Montezemolo, Luca, *1947-, Italian business executive, politician and entrepreneur*

De Amicis, Edmondo, *1846-1908, Italian writer and journalist*

de Maupassant, Guy, *1850-1893, French writer, poet, travel reporter and essayist*

Emiliani, Andrea, *1931-, Italian art historian*

Forster, Edward Morgan, *1879-1970, English writer*

Johnson, Samuel, *1709-1784, English literary critic, poet, essayist and biographer*

Maccari, Silvia, *n.d., Italian aphorist*

Marzotto, Marta, *1931-2016, Italian model, stylist and socialite*

Masters, Edgar Lee, *1868-1950, American poet, writer and lawyer*

Mastroianni, Marcello, *1924-1996, Italian actor*

Pasolini, Pier Paolo, *1922-1975, Italian poet, writer, director, actor, dramatist and journalist*

Piovene, Guido, *1907-1974, Italian writer and journalist*

Ponti, Gio, *1891-1979, Italian architect, designer and essayist*

I seemed to be reaching the heights
of art. And to breathe the air
that the masters breathed,
and to see the world with their eyes.

- Edgar Lee Masters -

It is not the union
of the light from the sky and
the sea that confers so much
ethereal luminosity, so much
sepulchral vitreous diaphaneity
on the cathedral of Trani: it is
the cathedral that makes the sea
luminous and the sky transparent,
revealing the ancient and eternal
dwellers, the little souls,
the heroes, the gods, the evil
spirits who dare not come near
her raised hand.

- Guido Ceronetti -

Naples' beauty grows day by day, week by week, as it reveals its secrets, until you understand that this is really the most beautiful bay of the world.

- Guido Piovene -

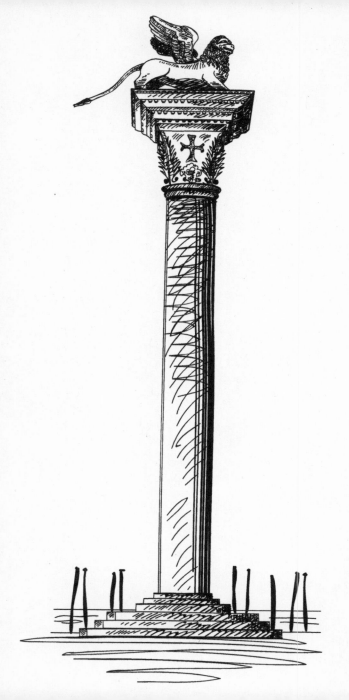

When I feel sad, I go back to Florence
to watch the dome by Brunelleschi:
if the genius of man is able to reach that,
then I can and must try to create,
to act, to live.

- Franco Zeffirelli -

There are cities whose beauty is immediately clear, cities that give themselves to everyone. And then there are other cities, secret cities, which love to be discovered.

Milan belongs to this kind, so much so that it is difficult to find the reasons for its appeal [...]. I believe that it consists in its "class," exactly as in certain women who are striking in their bearing, even if they are certainly not beautiful, or even made up.

- Carlo Castellaneta -

Trieste has a surly grace.
If one likes it, it is like a rascal,
harsh and voracious, with blue eyes
and hands too big to offer a flower.

- Umberto Saba -

*Italy has a great export:
its brand, its lifestyle, its taste.*

- Luca Cordero di Montezemolo -

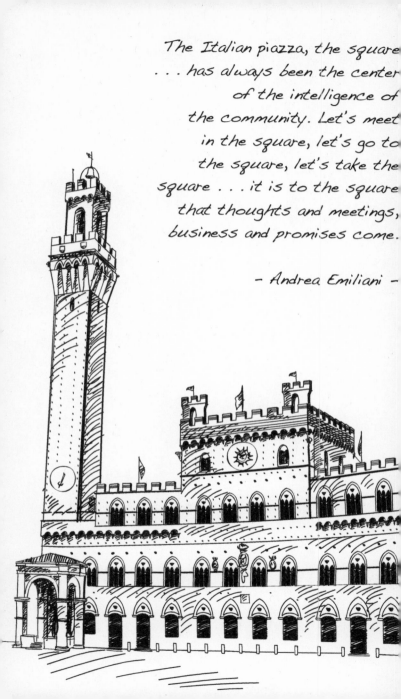

The Italian piazza, the square
. . . has always been the center
of the intelligence of
the community. Let's meet
in the square, let's go to
the square, let's take the
square . . . it is to the square
that thoughts and meetings,
business and promises come.

— Andrea Emiliani —

I'd love to live on a completely
Neapolitan planet, because
I know I'd be happy there.
Naples should be taken
as a unique, very intelligent city,
Naples is too special, so not
everyone can understand it . . .

– Marcello Mastroianni –

Verona, with its old walls
that surround it, its bridges
by crenellated parapets, its long,
wide streets, its memories
of the Middle Ages, has a large
air that commands respect.

- Paul Valéry -

One doesn't come to Italy for niceness.
[...] One comes for life.

- Edward Morgan Forster -

Rome is not like any other city.
It's a big museum, a living room
that shall be crossed on ones toes.

- Alberto Sordi -

I think Italy is a unique country. Come on, everyone envies us! We have pizza, we have pasta, we have Mediterranean flavors, beaches with crystal-clear water, and the scents of nature in the air. And then, we have love. We have it in our hearts, because more than ever we love everything around us: life, people, animals. I think the Italians represent the best of this splendid country.

- Silvia Maccari -

The Creator made Italy
from designs
by Michaelangelo.

- Mark Twain -

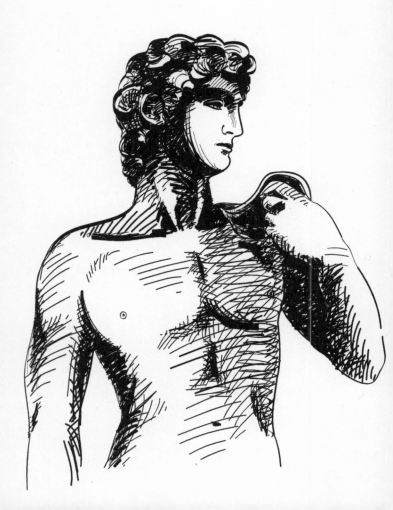

In 1937 I had two marvellous days at Assisi.
There, alone in the little twelfth century
Romanesque chapel of Santa Maria
degli Angeli, an incomparable marvel of purity
where Saint Francis often used to pray,
something stronger than I was compelled me
for the first time in my life
to go down on my knees.

- Simone Weil -

A man who has not been
in Italy, is always conscious
of an inferiority.

- Samuel Johnson -

I love your superb sea
and your sublime Alps.
I also love your solemn monuments
and your immortal memories;
I love your glory and your beauty.

– Edmondo De Amicis –

There are all the little, infinite,
innumerable city-states which
make up Italy; it is thus
a country unique in the world,
a country of an incredible beauty,
multiplicity and variety.
Italy is the country that enabled
the ancient world to become
modern. Italy is the country
where the Renaissance,
the critical re-thinking of the
ancient world, took place; it is through
an operation of this kind
that the ancient world
became modern.

- Giorgio Bassani -

Italy was half built
by God himself,
half by architects.

- Gio Ponti -

Venice! Is there a name in human language that make us dream most? Is there a city more admired, more celebrated, more sung by poets, more desired by lovers, more visited and more illustrious?

- Guy de Maupassant -

Perhaps the masterpiece of Apulia
is Alberobello . . . From the first wall
to the last, not a foreign body,
no plagiarism, not an expedient,
not a false note . . . The colors are
strictly white - a soft, cold white
with a few streaks of pale blue -
and carbon-black.

- Pier Paolo Pasolini -

You may have
the Universe
if I may have
Italy.

- Giuseppe Verdi -

I went every evening, around one
in the morning, to have another look
at the Cathedral. Lit up by a beautiful moon,
the church offers a vision of ravishing
beauty and one unique in this world.
Never has architecture given me
such sensations.

- Stendhal -

The names of the Risorgimento are alive,
they are within us, they belong to us.
Wherever I go, on this long journey
through Italy, I realize that Italians
are always proud of their history.

- Carlo Azeglio Ciampi -

Everything here breathes grandeur, style, humanity, purity and beauty, in the highest degree. I think I'd be happier here with you than anywhere else. This is the highest praise I can do to this city.

– Klemens von Metternich –

If you live in Rome, after a while
you are no longer aware of its beauty,
but as soon as you go away even for
a short trip and then return, you find
that Rome is more beautiful,
magical and magnificent than before.

- Marta Marzotto -

Italy, and the spring and first love all together should suffice to make the gloomiest person happy.

— Bertrand Russell —

_____

_____

_____

_____

_____

Everyone who has a dream
should go to Italy.
It doesn't matter if you think
your dream is dead and buried,
in Italy it will rise
and walk again.

- Elizabeth Spencer -

WHITE STAR PUBLISHERS